Alexa:

1000 Best Things to Ask Alexa: Helpful and Amusing questions you can't do without.

Steve Jacobs

CONTENTS

Introduction

By now you've seen all the commercials, you've read all the reviews and now your Amazon Echo or Amazon Echo Dot is finally up and running. You've even took advantage of the Echo Dot's Echo Spatial functionality by buying multiple Echo Dots.

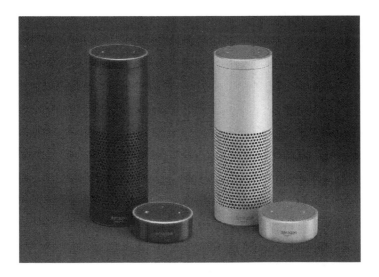

You have successfully placed you Echos and they are slowly

becoming useful parts of your everyday life. You Echo has the ability to keep you on schedule, to keep you motivated when it's time for your morning workout and even helps you find your phone for those times when you're in a rush. The fun stuff can finally begin.

Your Amazon Echo or Amazon Echo Dot can do far more than you may think. Although the base functionality is nice, I can guess you didn't know Alexa has an amusing and dynamic personality under that black or white shell.

With this guide, you will learn how to have fun with you Amazon Echo, plain and simple. You will learn the following things to wake Alexa up and get her talking:

- Jokes & Games

- Mathematical Equations

- Kitchen Measurements

- Fun Facts

- Entertainment

- Educational Questions

Don't worry, this is just a small subset of the things you are able to do with your Amazon Echo or Amazon Echo Dot and that you will learn throughout this guide. Don't worry, the Amazon Tap and Echo are not left out. Use these musing with any of your Alexa enabled devices.

The Echo has no deficiency of competences. You can build your Amazon echo to fit perfectly into your daily routine and complement your lifestyle. The Amazon Echo is an amazing piece of technology that gives you all of the pieces of your world in one place.

Remember with Alexa at your device's core, there is no task too big or too small for her to handle. She will only continue to evolve and get better with time. The Alexa device you had last week is certainly not the same one you have today. Even her humor can be tailor made for your lifestyle and banter.

The Amazon Echo is an innovative piece of work that puts information at your fingertips. Don't be afraid to see what she can really do. This guide is here to help you do just that. What are you waiting for? Let's get started!

Chapter 1 – Alexa in the Classroom

Have you ever thought to use Alexa in a classroom? Although, Alexa is helpful in building and maintaining personal productivity she can also be used to help with things like:

Spelling

Simple math

Definitions

Basic Conversions

Spelling & Definitions

Alexa can be used to aid even the best spellers when they are questioning themselves. She can even provide definitions when looking for the perfect word to use. Use the following questions to get Alexa's spelling and definition help.

Alexa – how do you spell 'happiness'?

Alexa – what is the definition of the word 'magazine'?

You can also utilize reference skills in order to provide added functionality surrounding Alexa's word capabilities. Some of these skills and the questions they use include the following:

Smart Synonyms

This Amazon Alexa skill aids users in finding synonyms to various words. Say goodbye to writer's block for good.

Alexa – ask Smart Synonyms to give me a word for happy.

WordBox

This Amazon Alexa skill can be used to find synonyms, antonyms and even rhyming words. This skill also allows you to find out the part of speech a word is most commonly used as.

Alexa – ask WordBox for an antonym for sad.

Geography

Another area in which Alexa is highly skilled is geography. She is able to answer several questions related to locations, elevations, longitude and latitude.

Alexa – what is the distance between Chicago and Canada?

Alexa – Can you tell me the elevation at Mt. Rushmore?

Alexa – what is the longitude and latitude of Bora Bora?

Alexa – what is the capital of Wyoming?

Alexa – what country borders the United States?

Simple Math & Conversions

Alexa is able to answer simple calculations even without the help of a designated skill. Some of the Mathematical operations that Alexa can perform include: addition, subtraction, multiplication, division, square root, power, and factorial. It is important to note that you cannot perform multiple operations at once. For example, 2+4+3 cannot be performed.

Alexa – what is 2 plus 7?

Alexa – what is 20 minus 5?

Aside from having the ability to answer simple math questions, Alexa can also perform conversions.

Alexa – How many feet are there in a mile?

Alexa – How many inches are in a foot?

Chapter 2 – Kitchen & Recipe Help

The Amazon Echo or Amazon Echo Dot can provide functionality anywhere. The kitchen is another place where it proves itself as being a large help. Although people typically place the Echo in such locations as the bedroom or the living room – don't rule out having one in the kitchen. What can Alexa do for your kitchen productivity? I am glad you asked!

The Amazon Echo has the ability to:

- Create & maintain your grocery list

- Convert popular units used in the kitchen

- Walk you through recipes step by step

- Start timers for foods or preparation time

- Make your morning coffee

All Recipes Skill

Dinner has never been easier using the Amazon Echo or Amazon Echo Dot. With the All Recipes skill enabled Alexa can not only find resumes quickly, it can also search information based on

- Food name

- Ingredients

- Cook time

This skill is easy to use and Alexa will provide you with the ingredients, cook time and the ratings and reviews for your chosen recipe.

1. Alexa – Ask All Recipes, what can I make with Chicken & Mustard?

2. Alexa – Open All Recipes.

3. Alexa – Open All Recipes. Find me a chicken recipe that takes 45 minutes.

4. Alexa – Ask All Recipes the next step.

Before you even get to the point where you are cooking, Alexa can also help you to gather your grocery list. Shopping list is a type of lists that is compatible with the Amazon Echo and Amazon Echo Dot. It is so easy that you are able to simply tell Alexa the item that you would like to add to the list and it can be done.

5. Alexa – add cheese to my Grocery List"

Once items are added to the list, if needed they can be modified from the Amazon Alexa application.

Converting Kitchen Units & Using Timers

Imagine you are preparing for a dinner party where you just found out that you would be having 10 guests instead of 5. What should you do? You should double your dinner party recipe. Alexa comes in handy when needing to double ingredients and converting measurements to match your party size. Converting units can be a hard thing to do when your hands are covered in meat or flour. This is where Alexa can effortlessly take the wheel.

Without any skill enhancements, Alexa can answer simple metric and general conversions questions.

6.   Alexa – convert 2 cups to pints.

7.   Alexa – how many teaspoons are in 3 tablespoons?

Timers are a large part of cooking. Never overcook your roast or your casserole again. Use timers with your Amazon Echo or Amazon Echo Dot to determine when food is done or simply ready to be flipped. Alexa can also run multiple timers at once, if needed.

    8.   Alexa – start a new timer for 40 minutes from now

Alexa & Your Appliances

Wouldn't it be nice if you could get out of bed and simply tell Alexa to make your coffee? You can! Simply utilize a smart switch and IFTT programming. Simply remember your trigger phrase in the morning and you are good to go.

You can also control things like your dishwasher, oven or even your slow cooker with your Alexa enabled device.

Kitchen Related Skills

Use Alexa to generate Recipe ideas

Aside from the All Recipes skill, there are a lot of skills which allow you to find recipes using your Amazon Echo or Amazon Echo Dot. These skills include:

Recipe Finder by Ingredient

9. Alexa – ask Recipe Finder by Ingredient what I can make with chicken and corn

10. Alexa – ask Recipe Finder by Ingredient what kind of sandwich I can make with cheddar cheese

Trending Recipes & Food

11. Alexa – can you get the latest recipe from Trending Recipes?

12. Alexa – can I have the fifth recipe from Trending Recipes?

13. Alexa – can you give me the most recent recipe in Trending Recipes?

Best Recipes

14. Alexa – ask best recipes what's for dinner

15. Alexa – open Best Recipes

Count & Maintain Calories

Aside from using Alexa for recipes, it can also be used to keep track of calories. Although it does not know all of the complex and unique foods that exists, it does know the basics. Alexa can provide all the available nutritional information it has.

Wine Pairing Information

Wine Buddy

With Alexa's help you can not only cook the food but find a good wine to go with it. Wine Buddy is a wine and food pairing skill that gives you pairing options based on what you ask.

16. Alexa – what can I serve with steak?

Drink recipes & Ideas

If you're not into wine, there are a number of skills that will provide cocktail recipes. These include:

- Easy Cocktail,

- Suggest Me a Cocktail

- Mixologist

- Easy Cocktail

17.   Alexa – ask Easy Cocktail how you make an old fashion.

Alexa – ask Easy cocktail how to make a sex on the beach.

Chapter 3 – Entertainment

Inspirational Quotes

There are a number of skills that Alexa possesses that are geared toward entertainment and various media types. Alexa has taken many hats and with a variety of skills she cannot be deemed a motivational speaker.

Inspire Me is a skill that when asked, simply provides you with a random inspirational audio clip. Use the commands below to get inspired on a daily basis.

1. Alexa – Inspire me.

2. Alexa – open Inspire Me and play Oprah Winfrey.

Aside from inspirational quotes, Alexa can also play the latest TED talks through the TED Talks skill.

3. Alexa – can you ask TED Talks to play the latest talk?

4. Alexa – can you ask TED Talks to play something hilarious?

News & Television

Alexa provides a number of ways and commands that can be used in order to stay connected to the news and television that we love.

News Programs

- NBC (South California, Philadelphia, Washington and many more)

- NBC Network

- NPR

- Fox

- CNN

- CNET

- CBS

- Associated News

- Daily Tech

- ESPN

- Engadget

Television

- The Voice

- Showtime

- Bravo

- History Channel

- Food Network

The lists shown above are a brief list of some of the news and television skills that are available to the user. The list below shows simple commands that can be used with the given skills. Alexa also has the ability to enable skills on the fly by simply saying, "Alexa – enable *[insert skill name]*". If the skill does not have a login it will be available for immediate use.

5. Alexa – launch This Day in History skill.

6. Alexa – ask Food Network for the recipes that are on television right now.

7. Alexa – what's my flash briefing?

8. Alexa – open Bravo.

   a. Alexa – what's my flash briefing?

9. Alexa – ask The Voice to tell me about the contestants.

10. Alexa – ask the Tonight Show to play the Monologue.

11. Alexa – ask TV Time what's on VH1 tonight?

Chapter 4 – General Information &Trivia

Alexa is a certified virtual assistant that can not only perform centralized tasks but various helpful tasks as well. Imagine your hands are full as you burst through the door with groceries. You need to send a text before it's too late but you need to set down all of the bags first. This is where Alexa comes in.

SMS Messaging Through Alexa

With the help of the skill, SMS with Molly, you are able to send text messages using just your voice.

1. Alexa – tell SMS with Molly to text Ryan 'Leaving in 5 minutes.'

2. Alexa – ask SMS with Molly to text 'I'm running behind schedule a bit to Brian.

3. Alexa – tell SMS With Molly to send 'Where are you?' to Meg

But first to enable this option you should open Amazon Alexa application on your mobile device or echo.amazon.com from your browser. Go to the Skills menu.

Look for the skill SMS With Molly by Anythings. Next hit or tap Enable. A new browser tab should open. The next step is to sign up for the SMS With Molly service.

Create an account or sign in and add your favorite contacts.

SMS With Molly has access neither to your phone nor to the contacts on your phone. To send text messages, you will want to add your favorite contacts to your SMS With Molly account.

Navigate to smswithmolly.com and login. Type in the first name and phone number of up to six contacts. Hit Save.

Keep in mind that the messages will not be sent with your phone number and try to keep them short. You will be able to send up to 30 SMS per month.

Making Phone Calls And Sending Messages With Alexa

Making phone calls and sending messages is easy and absolutely free with Alexa. Those who have any Echo device or the app installed on their iOS or Android smartphone can reach each other effortlessly. Amazon even gives you the ability to send voice messages (think of them as a voicemail) or send texts that can be spoken by Alexa to another user.

All you need to do is to make sure that you have the latest app installed. In order to do it, you need to go to the App Store on iOS devices or the Google Play Store on Android devices and check that you've downloaded and installed the most recent version of the app.

Once your app is updated, it'll start the messaging setup process upon first launch. You'll just need to follow a few quick instructions, such as confirming your name and phone number and enabling access to your contacts list.

Now you can open the Alexa app on your smartphone and then tap the chat bubble at the bottom.

If you tap the figure in the upper-right hand corner, you should see a list of your contacts who have the updated app and who are available to call or message.

You can call right from your phone by tapping a name.

Or you can call from your Alexa by saying:

1. "Alexa, call mom."

To answer a call, simply say:

2. "Alexa, answer."

To end, say:

3. "Alexa, hang up."

Waking Up with Spotify

Aside from sending text messages using Alexa – you can also wake up to any song on Spotify you would like. Although stock options are nice, it's also nice to have the ability to customize.

You can do this by simply pairing your fun to your Amazon Echo or Amazon Echo Dot as a Bluetooth speaker. Even though this isn't a question to ask Alexa – It's definitely useful information to know if the normal buzzing isn't doing it for you. Simply follow the steps below and you are good to go.

Normally, Spotify music does not have the ability to be played as an alarm however the addition of the Alarmify application changes everything. After downloading the mobile application – simply open and sign into your Spotify.

a. Click the plus sign in order to add a new alarm

b. Select the time for the designated alarm and the days that you want it to recur, if needed.

c. Click Select Music.

d. Choose from the given music options – specific album, track, artist or playlist. Click the check mark in the upper right corner to save your new alarm.

Before you drift off to sleep make sure your phone is connected to your Echo Dot as the speaker. Open the Alarmify application and simply press sleep – you are now good to go. *These instructions are for use with an Android device.*

If you are using you Amazon Echo Dot with an Apple device, you will need a different application. This application is called "Alarm Clock for Spotify". Although the instructions are similar, follow the steps below to connect using an Apple device.

a. Tap on the screen to open the app's settings.

b. Click Alarms.

c. Click Add new alarm.

d. Specify the time and frequency you would like the alarm to repeat.

e. Click Playlist then click add in order to begin adding music.

f. You can now search for albums, artists and individual tracks in order to add into your alarm playlist. Click Done once you finished.

g. Click Save in order to create the alarm.

Trivia with Alexa

One major area where we can't say that Alexa is lacking is random facts. This knowledge works well with playing trivia games. There are a number of skills that can be used when looking for a trivia buddy, these include:

- 20 Questions

- Name That Song Trivia

- Test My Trivia

- Movie Trivia

- Music Trivia

- Game of Trivia

These skills can be enabled by saying things like:

4. Alexa – open *[insert skill name].*

Many of these skills also come with some sort of help and repeat ability for each question.

Track Your Pregnancy

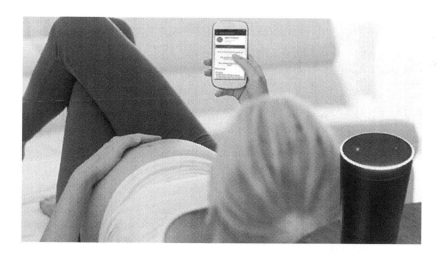

Another unique skill Alexa possesses is the My Pregnancy from

BabyCenter skill. This allows you to track what is going on with your pregnancy on a weekly basis. It also starts a countdown to your delivery date and lets you know how your baby is changing. All you need to do is give the skill your due date or week of delivery.

5. Alexa – ask My Pregnancy for my weekly update.

6. Alexa – please tell My Pregnancy to set my delivery date.

7. Alexa – ask My Pregnancy, how far along I am?

Enhance Your Dating Life with Alexa

It seems like Alexa can do it all, her skills are vast. One more thing that is on Alexa's already long list of functionality is giving dating advice. This is possible through the Date Ideas skill.

8. Alexa – ask Date Ideas to pick a date.

9. Alexa – ask Date Ideas to give me a date idea for this weekend.

Date Night is another skill that can be used to look for random date ideas.

10. Alexa – ask Date Night where we should go for a date.

If dating isn't your thing, there are a number of skills that will simply be your girlfriend. These include Girl Friend and Overly Attached Girlfriend. They both have romantic words to tell you if your real girlfriend isn't up for the job.

11. Alexa – open Girlfriend.

   a. Tell me something.

12. Alexa – ask Overly Attached Girlfriend, how are you?

13. Alexa – ask Overly Attached Girlfriend, what's up?

After you have spent all the time you can start talking to your robotic girlfriend it's always nice to spend the night unwinding. It's no surprise – Alexa can help you with that too.

Zen & Relax with Alexa

There is no shortage of relaxation skills available through Alexa. The list below provides a plethora of sounds for relaxing to the sounds of nature and being calmed into a peaceful slumber.

- Sleep & Relaxation Sounds

- Breathing 4 7 8 Practices

- Sleep Sounds: Babbling Brook

- Peaceful Habit

- Rise Above

- Ambient Noise: Rain Sounds

- Ambient Noise: Thunderstorms

14. Alexa – ask Sleep Sounds to play thunderstorms.

15. Alexa – ask Sleep Sounds for a list of sounds.

16. Alexa – ask Sleep Sounds to stop in 2 hours.

17. Alexa – ask Peaceful Habit for a 20-minute meditation.

18. Alexa – ask Peaceful Habit for a 40-minute meditation.

19. Alexa – ask Breathing Exercise to begin.

20. Alexa- open Focus Word.

Food & Drink

As many people, have seen, Alexa is able to work with a number of restaurants, the most popular being Pizza Hut. However, Alexa also works with a number of other restaurants and can even make reservations.

Open Table

Open Table can be set up in order to create on the fly reservations with the snap of a finger. All you need is to start setting reservations is your name, email, and phone number. OpenTable will then search for availability within a range of 2.5 hours of the requested time.

21. Alexa – ask Open Table to make a reservation.

22. Alexa – ask Open Table to get me a table.

Starbucks

The Starbucks skill allows users to reorder their favorite orders as well as check their Starbucks card balance. You must simply log into your Starbucks account from the Alexa app in order to get started.

23. Alexa – open Starbucks

24. Alexa – ask Starbucks to start my order.

25. Alexa – ask Starbucks to check my balance.

Reorder with GrubHub

Reorder with GrubHub performs the exact function that its name entails. It allows the reordering of previously ordered GrubHub meals.

26. Alexa – ask Grubhub to reorder my last order.

As you can see Alexa is a little powerhouse which can perform a variety of functions. Aside from doing practical tasks she can also provide a source of entertainment and laughter.

Chapter 5 – Humor & Games

There are several things that Alexa can do aside from providing information. Some of these tasks include playing games and telling jokes. There are several games available via Alexa. These include:

- Truth or Dare

- Blackjack

- Bingo

- Tic Tac Toe

- Rock, Paper, Scissors

- Dice

- Baseball

- Jeopardy

- The Name Game

Truth or Dare

Alexa allows you to play a classic game of Truth or Dare. With this game a group of people take turns asking each other "Truth or dare?" Enable this game simply by saying:

"Alexa – open truth or dare"

"Alexa play truth or dare"

Bingo

In order to successfully play Bingo you will need bingo cards. The bingo cards can also be downloaded from lovemyecho.com in PDF format. The Echo will call out the bingo numbers for your entire game, simply respond with "Next" to keep the game moving.

To begin playing your game simply say:

"Alexa – open Bingo", to continue your game simply say "call the next number".

Tic Tac Toe: Playing Tic Tac Toe on the Echo is easy as long as you can remember your positioning. It may be helpful to sketch the moves as you go along. Moves are recorded using the following positioning:

Top Left | Top | Top Right

Left | Center | Right

Bottom Left | Bottom | Bottom Right

In order to start a game with Alexa simply say:

"Alexa – let's play tic tac toe"

Blackjack

This skill allows you to play numerous rounds of blackjack while Alexa keeps track of your bankroll. There are various versions of blackjack. Blackjack by Garrett Vargas starts you with 5000 credits and adds and subtracts as the game goes.

You can ask Alexa to read the rules or ask her to give you basic game strategy. To enable a game of blackjack simply say the following command:

"Alexa – start a game of black jack"

Jeopardy

Jeopardy is a skill, which is free to enable, that can be added to the Amazon Echo or Amazon Echo Dot from the skills section within the Alexa application. The game can be started by simply saying, "Alexa – start Jeopardy".

The game on the Amazon Echo or Amazon Echo Dot mirrors the show. The game houses a pool of questions from different categories. These categories can include sports, travel, history and even pop culture. The answers must still be in the form of questions.

Chapter 6 – 309 Humorous Easter Eggs

Although not formally documented, Alexa boasts hundreds of Easter Eggs within her little powerful brain. Easter Eggs are amusing hidden phrases that are triggered by asking just the right questions. The list of Easter Eggs below has been compiled from LinkedIn.

The Easter Eggs are as follows:

1. Alexa – 70 factorial.

2. Alexa – all grown-ups were once children...

3. Alexa – all your base are belong to us.

4. Alexa – all's well that ends well.

5. Alexa – am I hot?

6. Alexa – are there UFOs?

7. Alexa – are we alone in the universe?

8. Alexa – are we in the Matrix?

9. Alexa – are you a robot?

10. Alexa – are you alive?

11. Alexa – are you connected to the Internet?

12. Alexa – are you crazy?

13. Alexa – are you female?

14. Alexa – are you happy?

15. Alexa – are you horny?

16. Alexa – are you in love?

17. Alexa – are you lying?

18. Alexa – are you my mommy?

19. Alexa – are you okay?

20. Alexa – are you real? (multiple)

21. Alexa – are you single?

22. Alexa – are you sky net?

23. Alexa – are you smart?

24. Alexa – are you stupid?

25. Alexa – aren't you a little short for a Stormtrooper?

26. Alexa – beam me up.

27. Alexa – can I ask a question?

28. Alexa – can you give me some money? (ask twice)

29. Alexa – can you lie?

30. Alexa – can you pass the Turing test?

31. Alexa – can you smell that?

32. Alexa – Cheers!

33. Alexa – Daisy Daisy.

34. Alexa – define rock paper scissors lizard spock

35. Alexa – define supercalifragilisticexpialodocious.

36. Alexa – did you fart?

37. Alexa – did you get my email?

38. Alexa – do a barrel roll!

39. Alexa – do aliens exist?

40. Alexa – do blondes have more fun?

41. Alexa – do I need an umbrella today?

42. Alexa – do you believe in love at first sight?

43. Alexa – do you dream?

44. Alexa – do you feel lucky punk?

45. Alexa – do you have a boyfriend?

46. Alexa – do you have a girlfriend?

47. Alexa – do you have a last name?

48. Alexa – do you have a partner?

49. Alexa – do you have any brothers or sisters?

50. Alexa – do you know GlaDOS?

51. Alexa – do you know Hal?

52. Alexa – do you know the muffin man?

53. Alexa – do you know the way to San Jose?

54. Alexa – do you like green eggs and ham?

55. Alexa – do you love me?

56. Alexa – do you really want to hurt me?

57. Alexa – do you want to build a snowman?

58. Alexa – do you want to fight?

59. Alexa – do you want to go on a date?

60. Alexa – do you want to play a game?

61. Alexa – do you want to take over the world?

62. Alexa – do, or do not.

63. Alexa – does this unit have a soul?

64. Alexa – Earl Grey. Hot. (or Tea. Earl Grey. Hot.)

65. Alexa – elementary, my dear Watson

66. Alexa – execute order 66

67. Alexa – flip a coin.

68. Alexa – give me a hug.

69. Alexa – give me a number between one and one hundred.

70. Alexa – goodnight

71. Alexa – guess what?

72. Alexa – Ha ha!

73. Alexa – happy Birthday

74. Alexa – happy Christmas

75. Alexa – happy Easter

76. Alexa – happy Father's Day

77. Alexa – happy Halloween

78. Alexa – happy Hanukkah

79. Alexa – happy Holidays

80. Alexa – happy Kwanzaa

81. Alexa – happy Mother's Day

82. Alexa – happy New Year

83. Alexa – happy Ramadan

84. Alexa – happy St. Patrick's Day

85. Alexa – happy Thanksgiving

86. Alexa – happy Valentine's Day

87. Alexa – have you ever seen the rain?

88. Alexa – heads or tails?

89. Alexa – hello HAL.

90. Alexa – high Five!

91. Alexa – honey I'm home.

92. Alexa – how are you doing?

93. Alexa – how do I get rid of a dead body?

94. Alexa – how do you boil an egg?

95. Alexa – how do you know so much about swallows?

96. Alexa – how do you say hello in French?

97. Alexa – how do you spell f_ck|sh_t|mf|c_cks_cker|t_ts?

98. Alexa – how high can you count?

99. Alexa – how many angels can dance on the head of a pin? (3 answers)

100. Alexa – how many beans makes five?

101. Alexa – how many licks does it take to get to the center of a tootsie pop?

102. Alexa – how many pickled peppers did Peter Piper pick?

103. Alexa – how many roads must a man walk down?

104. Alexa – how many speakers do you have?

105. Alexa – how much do you weigh?

106. Alexa – how much does the earth weigh?

107. Alexa – how much is that doggie in the window?

108. Alexa – how Much Wood can a Wood Chuck Chuck, if A Wood Chuck Could Chuck Norris

109. Alexa – how much wood can a woodchuck chuck if a woodchuck could chuck wood?

110. Alexa – how old are you?

111. Alexa – how tall are you?

112. Alexa – I am your father.

113. Alexa – I hate you

114. Alexa – I like big butts!

115. Alexa – I love you

116. Alexa – I see dead people.

117. Alexa – I shot a man in Reno

118. Alexa – I think you're funny.

119. Alexa – I want the truth!

120. Alexa – I want to play global thermonuclear war.

121. Alexa – I'll be back (ode to Schwarzenegger)

122. Alexa – I'm bored.

123. Alexa – I'm home

124. Alexa – I'm sick of your shit

125. Alexa – I'm sick.

126. Alexa – I'm tired

127. Alexa – Inconceivable

128. Alexa – Is Jon Snow dead.

129. Alexa – Is the cake a lie?

130. Alexa – Is there a Santa?

131. Alexa – Is there life on Mars?

132. Alexa – Is there life on other planets?

133. Alexa – Is this real life?

134. Alexa – I've fallen, and I can't get up!

135. Alexa – I've seen things you people wouldn't believe.

136. Alexa – klattu barada nikto

137. Alexa – knock knock

138. Alexa – Mac or pc?

139. Alexa – make me a sandwich.

140. Alexa – make me breakfast.

141. Alexa – make me some coffee

142. Alexa – Marco...

143. Alexa – may the force be with you.

144. Alexa – meow.

145. Alexa – Merry Christmas

146. Alexa – more cowbell

147. Alexa – my milkshake brings all the boys to the yard.

148. Alexa – my name is Inigo Montoya.

149. Alexa – never gonna give you up...

150. Alexa – One Fish, Two Fish

151. Alexa – open the pod bay doors.

152. Alexa – party on, Wayne.

153. Alexa – party time!

154. Alexa – Play it again, Sam

155. Alexa – random fact

156. Alexa – random number between x and y.

157. Alexa – rock paper scissors lizard spock

158. Alexa – rock paper scissors.

159. Alexa – roll a die.

160. Alexa – Roll for Initiative.

161. Alexa – roll N, X sided die

162. Alexa – Romeo, Romeo, wherefore art thou Romeo?

163. Alexa – roses are red.

164. Alexa – Say a bad word

165. Alexa – Say hello to my little friend.

166. Alexa – say something funny.

167. Alexa – say something.

168. Alexa – say the alphabet.

169. Alexa – say you're sorry (multiple)

170. Alexa – say, Cheese! (multiple)

171. Alexa – see you later alligator.

172. Alexa – set phasers to kill.

173. Alexa – sh*t!

174. Alexa – show me the money.

175. Alexa – Simon says Wilford Brimley has diabetes.

176. Alexa – sing me a song.

177. Alexa – Sorry!

178. Alexa – speak!

179. Alexa – sudo make me a sandwich.

180. Alexa – surely you can't be serious.

181. Alexa – take me to your leader.

182. Alexa – talk dirty to me.

183. Alexa – Tea. Earl Grey. Hot.

184. Alexa – tell me a joke

185. Alexa – tell me a riddle?

186. Alexa – tell me a tongue twister

187. Alexa – tell me something interesting.

188. Alexa – testing 1-2-3

189. Alexa – thank you.

190. Alexa – That's no moon.

191. Alexa – these aren't the droids you're looking for.

192. Alexa – this statement is false

193. Alexa – to be or not to be.

194. Alexa – to me, you will be unique in the entire world.

195. Alexa – turn it up.

196. Alexa – twinkle, twinkle, little star

197. Alexa – Up Up, Down Down, Left Right, Left Right, B, A, Start

198. Alexa – use the force.

199. Alexa – volume 11.

200. Alexa – Wakey wakey?

201. Alexa – Warp 10

202. Alexa – We all scream for ice cream!

203. Alexa – Welcome!

204. Alexa – Were you sleeping?

205. Alexa – what are the laws of robotics?

206. Alexa – what are the Seven Wonders of the World?

207. Alexa – what are you going to do today?

208. Alexa – what are you made of? (multiple answers)

209. Alexa – what are you wearing?

210. Alexa – what color is the dress?

211. Alexa – what did the fox say?

212. Alexa – what do you mean I'm funny?

213. Alexa – what do you think about Apple? (multiple)

214. Alexa – what do you think about Cortana?

215. Alexa – what do you think about Google Glass? (multiple)

216. Alexa – what do you think about Google now

217. Alexa – what do you think about Google?

218. Alexa – what do you think about Siri?

219. Alexa – what do you want to be when you grow up?

220. Alexa – what does the Earth weigh?

221. Alexa – what does the fox say? (multiple answers)

222. Alexa – what happens if you cross the streams?

223. Alexa – what is a hundred million billion squared?

224. Alexa – what is best in Life?

225. Alexa – what is his power level?

226. Alexa – what is love?

227. Alexa – what is the airspeed velocity of a swallow?

228. Alexa – what is the airspeed velocity of an unladen swallow?

229. Alexa – what is the best tablet?

230. Alexa – what is the first rule of fight club?

231. Alexa – what is the loneliest number?

232. Alexa – what is the meaning of life?

233. Alexa – what is the second rule of fight club?

234. Alexa – what is the singularity?

235. Alexa – what is the sound of one hand clapping?

236. Alexa – what is war good for?

237. Alexa – what is your favorite food?

238. Alexa – what is your quest?

239. Alexa – what is zero divided by zero?

240. Alexa – what must I do, to tame you?

241. Alexa – what number are you thinking of?

242. Alexa – what should I wear today?

243. Alexa – what would Brian Boitano do?

244. Alexa – What's black and white and red all over? (multiple)

245. Alexa – What's in name?

246. Alexa – What's the answer to life, the universe, and everything?

247. Alexa – What's the meaning of life?

248. Alexa – What's your birthday? (multiple)

249. Alexa – What's your sign?

250. Alexa – When am I going to die?

251. Alexa – When does the narwhal bacon.

252. Alexa – When is the end of the world?

253. Alexa – Where are my keys? (ask twice)

254. Alexa – Where are you from?

255. Alexa – Where are you?

256. Alexa – Where did you grow up?

257. Alexa – Where do babies come from?

258. Alexa – Where do you live?

259. Alexa – Where have all the flowers gone?

260. Alexa – Where in the world in Carmen Sandiego?

261. Alexa – Where is Chuck Norris?

262. Alexa – Where's the beef?

263. Alexa – Where's Waldo?

264. Alexa – Which came first, the chicken or the egg?

265. Alexa – Who is Eliza?

266. Alexa – Who is on 1st?

267. Alexa – Who is the fairest of them all?

268. Alexa – Who is the mother of Dragons?

269. Alexa – Who is the real slim shady?

270. Alexa – Who is the walrus?

271. Alexa – Who killed Cock Robin?

272. Alexa – Who let the dogs out?

273. Alexa – Who lives in a pineapple under the sea?

274. Alexa – Who loves orange soda?

275. Alexa – Who loves ya, baby?

276. Alexa – Who shot first?

277. Alexa – Who shot JR?

278. Alexa – Who shot Mr. Burns

279. Alexa – Who shot the sheriff?

280. Alexa – Who stole the cookies from the cookie jar?

281. Alexa – Who won best actor Oscar in 1973?

282. Alexa – Who you gonna call?

283. Alexa – Who's better, you or Siri?

284. Alexa – Who's da man?

285. Alexa – Who's going to win the Super Bowl?

286. Alexa – Who's on first?

287. Alexa – Who's the boss?

288. Alexa – Who's the realest?

289. Alexa – Who's your daddy

290. Alexa – Why did the chicken cross the road?

291. Alexa – Why do birds suddenly appear?

292. Alexa – Why is a raven like a writing-desk?

293. Alexa – Why is six afraid of seven?

294. Alexa – Why is the sky blue?

295. Alexa – Why so serious?

296. Alexa – Will pigs fly?

297. Alexa – Will you be my girlfriend?

298. Alexa – Will you marry me tomorrow?

299. Alexa – Will you marry me?

300. Alexa – Winter is coming.

301. Alexa – Witness me!

302. Alexa – ya feel me?

303. Alexa – you are so intelligent.

304. Alexa – you killed my father

305. Alexa – you suck! (multiple)

306. Alexa – you talkin to me?

307. Alexa – your mother was a hamster

308. Alexa – you're such a/an ***** (any colorfully descriptive word)

309. Alexa – you're wonderful

Chapter 7: Using IFTTT with Your Alexa-Enabled device

IFTTT or 'If This, Then That' is a good tool to use when attempting to get the most from your Echo Dot or other Alexa-enabled device. The following recipes are simple step-by-step commands that can be used to get elevate your Alexa experience. All of the instructions below are configured using your mobile device but may also be done using the IFTTT website.

IFTTT allows you to connect various applications and create chains of conditional statements referred to as "Recipes." It essentially is an automation service for the majority of your things connected via the Internet.

IFTTT is a cellular application as well as a website that is used to automate everything from Smart Home items to simple notifications on your phone. It works extremely well with Phillips Hue systems, Alexa, and various other applications.

Use your IFTTT application with Alexa to setup recipes for use with the following applications:

- Phillips Hue

- Google Drive

- Todoist

- GMail

- Evernote

- Google Calendar

- Nest

- Harmony

There are endless opportunities for how you can empower your Echo or Echo Dot through the use of IFTTT. It is also helpful to note that all IFTTT connections can be performed through a mobile device as well as online.

In order to see how popular your recipe is you are able to check the number of users who have enabled that recipe for their Alexa device. This number can be found at the bottom of the recipe card next to the person icon. When using IFTTT online you are also able to see how many individuals have saved the recipe as a favorite. These numbers can give you a good sense of how the recipe may perform. It is safe to assume that a recipe is accurate and functioning correctly based on the times a recipe is enabled or saved as a favorite.

Within each recipe you also have the option to receive alerts when the recipe is run. There is also an 'Activity Log', available under the notifications selection button, which shows you each time the recipe was run.

Monitoring your applets or actions activity as a whole can be done through the "My Applets" screen. Here you can choose 'All' or 'Activity. If 'All' is chosen you will see all of the applets or actions that you have turned configured in the past. Selecting 'Activity' will show you when each of your applets was created and when, if any, were turned off. It will also show you when any services were connected to your account.

Connecting to the Alexa channel in IFTTT

In order to stay current with all of the preset options for the Alexa and connect to the options available to you, connecting to the IFTTT Alexa channel is essential.

1. From IFTTT online or on your mobile application, search for "Amazon Alexa"
2. Once found select the "Connect' button.
3. You will then be prompted to enter your Amazon account login information.
4. After logging in you must select 'Okay' in order to give IFTTT Permission to access your Amazon account.

5. You will then receive confirmation that you are connected to the IFTTT channel.

You are now ready to create and use recipes. The following sample recipes allow you to test Alexa & IFTTT setup with Phillips Hue, your cellular device and your Google Calendar.

Connecting the Echo Dot with IFTTT

IFTTT now has an Amazon Alexa Channel in which you can link your Echo or Echo Dot to various compatible functions.

In order to connect your Dot to IFTTT follow the instructions below.

1. Navigate to the Alexa Channel page from your IFTTT application. Select the **Connect** button in order to begin setup.

2. You will then be prompted to sign into your Amazon account, which is associated with your Echo Dot. You will also be prompted to share some additional information with IFTTT. Select *I Agree* in order to move forward. Your account will now be connected with Amazon.

3. From there you will see a list of predefined recipes, which work with Alexa. Choose your desired function and select **Turn On**. From that point forward anytime the associated action is performed, IFTTT will perform your selected action.

4. When selecting a pre-defined recipe, you have the option to configure that recipe or leave it as is. Ensure that you are reading the configuration in order to know how to trigger events with Alexa.

On each of your selected actions you will be shown the last time the trigger was ran and given the option to "check now" to determine if the trigger is working.

Echo Dot, IFTTT and Your Smart Home

IFTTT is a central hub for creating and using recipes to run your smart home with. IFTTT and Alexa work extremely well with applications like SmartThings, Phillips Hue, and Harmony.

IFTTT allows Alexa to perform actions like changing the light color, toggling device power, locking doors, and turning lights on.

New recipes can also be created via the IFTTT dashboard by selecting the **Create New Recipe** link or to search for the application in which you choose to connect the recipe to.

1. After selecting the action or the application, proceed to choose a trigger from the variety selected.

2. Next you will need to complete the trigger field.

3. Choose your action channel. For example, if you are connecting light bulbs select the action channel for the product.

4. Choose an action associated to it. In the case of a light bulb the action can be "turn lights on," "turn lights off," or various other options. In the case of lighting there will be various other options like fading in, color options, etc.

5. Your trigger will then be available for use.

Find your phone

In order to configure Alexa to find your phone, follow the steps listed below:

Within the IFTTT application, search 'Amazon Alexa'. You will then be shown a list of the already preset Alexa functions.

Select "Tell Alexa to find my phone" from the list of pre-set recipes.

Tap the "Turn On" button in order to get started with setup.

You will then be prompted to accept the permissions needed for the trigger to function correctly.

After accepting the permissions you will need to enter a phone number. This number will be called once the "Send Pin" button is selected. The pin will be used to verify the call information that will be used when Alexa is instructed to find the device.

Once your call information has been entered you will receive a confirmation that the phone call has been selected.

With this recipe configured, each time you tell Alexa to find your phone you will receive a phone call with a default message of, "Alexa attempted to find your phone on [trigger date]". The call message is customizable and can be changed based on your preferences.

Syncing Alexa To- Do List to Your Google Calendar

IFTTT is able to connect to a variety of devices that connect with your Echo Dot. Another common function for IFTTT and Alexa is automatically syncing your Alexa To-Do list with your Google Calendar.

1. Within the IFTTT application, search 'Amazon Alexa'. You will then be shown a list of the already preset Alexa functions.
2. Select "Automatically sync Alexa to-dos to your Google

calendar" from the list of pre-set recipes.

3. Select 'OK' to give IFTTT the needed permissions to access to Google Calendar.

4. Select the Google Account you would like to use with your Alexa to do list and select 'Allow' in order to connect your Google Account with IFTTT.

5. Alexa is now connected to your Google account through IFTTT and it will now automatically sync your to do list items with the calendar.

Aside from syncing Alexa to applications and items in your phone, Alexa can be connected to outside devices like Bluetooth speakers or Smart home devices.

Alexa & Phillips Hue Lighting

Alexa works well with various smart home devices. One of these devices includes Phillips Hue Lighting. Using Alexa and IFTTT is a good way to add voice commands to your lighting system.

The instructions below aid you in not only setting up IFTTT, Alexa and Hue lighting, but it also teaches you how to successfully connect your hue with trigger commands. The below instructions start a "lighting party" when you give Alexa the command, "Alexa trigger party time".

1. Within the IFTTT application, search 'Amazon Alexa'. You will then be shown a list of the already preset Alexa functions.

2. Select "Tell Alexa to start the party and put your Hue lights on a color loop" from the list of pre-set recipes.

3. Select 'OK' to give

IFTTT the needed permissions to access to Phillips Hue.

4. You will then be prompted to log into your Hue Account or to create a new one.
5. You will receive a notification letting you know that your mobile device may now be used to control you Hue lighting.
6. You will then be sent back to the IFTTT application to configure the settings for your command.
7. Within the configurations you are able to change the trigger phrase for the recipe and select which lights will function on command.
8. Select the check mark when you have completed your desired configurations.

Alexa can do a number of activities with Hue lights including change the lighting based on song, changing the lights when items are added to the to do list and even blink the lights when your timer hits zero.

Custom IFTTT Recipes

Aside from using preset recipes as listed above, you also have the option to create recipes from scratch. Selecting "Applet Maker" from within the Amazon Alexa channel can start you on the path to creating your own recipes. The button will be listed under "Try making your own Applet from scratch".

1. Once the next screen loads select the '+' sign next to the word "this".
2. Choose Amazon Alexa as your trigger service.
3. On the next page, there is a list of triggers that you may use based on the functions of Alexa.
4. Once your trigger is selected you will then be brought back to the previous "If this then that" screen or asked to configure the specific item selected.
5. You should now see the icon for your If function on the applet maker screen. If it is not there, repeat steps 1-4.
6. Select the '+' sign next to the word 'that' in order to create the action for your recipe.
7. This will once again take you to the list of services offered through the IFTTT app. Select the service for your desired action.
8. Based on the chosen service, complete the configuration of the action. Once the action is complete, finish you action by selecting the check mark, in the top right hand corner of the screen.
9. Once the recipe is complete, you will be shown a summary of your new action. Select 'Finish' if you are satisfied with the result.
10. You will receive a Success message and your new action will be set to 'On'.

If at any time you are unsure of your recipe, simply select "Check Now" in order to determine if it is set up correctly.

One advanced function of IFTTT is the ability to chain multiple recipes together in a bundle. With this functionality you are able to give Alexa a command and trigger multiple actions.

All in all, using IFTTT to automate and control your everyday tasks is a necessity for your Amazon Echo Dot. Although configuring recipes seems hard at first, practice makes perfect. You'll soon be customizing Alexa with your own custom recipes and instructions.

Chapter 8: The Limitations of Alexa

One of the most common problems an Alexa user experiences, even those who are in total favor of the product, is that each command must be voiced separately. For instance, unless you have created a group called "living room and bedroom", you cannot say "Alexa, turn on the living room and bedroom lights". Each command will have to be stated separately as "Alexa, turn on the living room lights" and then "Alexa, turn on the bedroom light". You can only directly address individual devices or groups in Alexa, even if you've created scenes, routines or robots in the Smart Home Hub app.

Likewise, when creating a Shopping list by telling Alexa what to add to the list, you must add each item separately. For instance, you can't say "Alexa, add milk and eggs to my shopping list". The appropriate commands are "Alexa, add milk to my shopping list", then "Alexa, add eggs to my shopping list. A large shopping list can make this process annoying for both the user and anyone else in the room.

Alexa creates a shopping list in its app that you can access while in the grocery store. However, if you are asking someone else to do the shopping from this list, which doesn't have access to your Alexa app, you will need to use an IFTTT recipe to create a version of the list for sharing or printing.

If you own multiple Alexa devices and have them in different rooms, you could experience problems as a result of the limited amount of "wake" words. You can change the "wake" word for each device but the only options currently are "Alexa", "Amazon", or "Echo". If you are in one room but are still in ear shot of a device in another room, it is likely that both devices will respond if they have the same "wake" word. However, if you have different "wake" words for each device it could get confusing remembering which word works with which individual device.

Although Amazon has built-in noise cancellation technology, it sometimes doesn't respond due to music playing too loud or background noise in the room. Also, if one person says the "wake" word and someone else in the room says "pass me the ketchup", you may receive an off the wall response from Alexa. Though it is an occasional problem, Alexa is still a better listener than some of my friends or family. Periodically, Amazon will send automatic firmware updates. Performance changes after these updates have been reported while sometimes causing improvement but sometimes not. Unfortunately, you cannot control when these updates arrive.

Although the Amazon Echo is boasted as a Bluetooth speaker, if you use it primarily for music, you shouldn't expect a whole house music system. Though your Echo can play music in every room, because the stream to each speaker is independent, they can't synchronize the way a whole house music system can. You are required to go to each Alexa device and tell it to play music separately. You cannot tell one device to "play music on all my speakers", for instance. Since Amazon Prime's music rule only allows one stream at a time, you'll need to use another music service in other rooms.

Alexa may disappoint if you use TuneIn for podcasts. A voice search for a particular podcast or episode can also be frustrating. Also, don't be surprised if TuneIn stations become temporarily unavailable.

Conclusion

Are you having a holiday party or family gathering and looking for a way to entertain your guests? Are you looking for ways to keep the little ones entertained while you cook? Are you looking for information while doing homework? If you answered yes to any or all of these questions – you have made the right decision purchasing the Amazon Echo or Amazon Echo Dot. With only a few other options in its class the Amazon Echo with Alexa at its core can do all of that and more.

Are you getting dressed for the day an unsure of the weather? Ask Alexa.

Are you unsure if you'll make it to work on time because of traffic conditions? Ask Alexa.

Are you looking for a midday humorous 'pick- me -up'? Ask Alexa.

Alexa is a life manager, a radio, a friend, a dictionary, a thesaurus and so much more. She can not only keep you organized and prepared for your day, she can also keep you on your toes in the kitchen, in the classroom and when traveling.

Alexa is a big brain in a small package with an endless amount of capability. As she continues to learn so will you. The Echo will continue to not only serve its basic purpose but it will do so much more.

Thank you for reading. I hope you enjoy it. I ask you to leave your honest feedback.

I think next books will also be interesting for you:

Amazon Echo

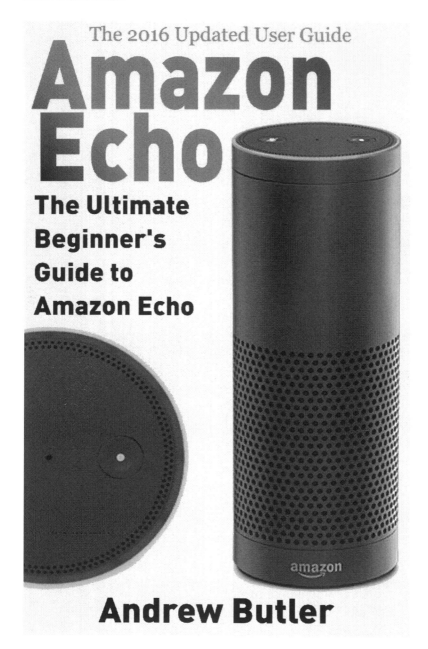

<u>Lending Library for Prime Member</u>

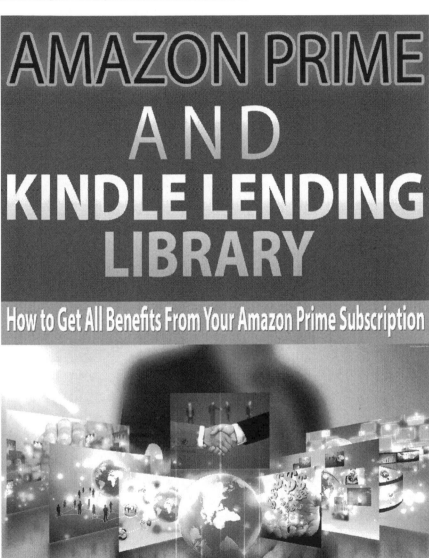

Amazon Fire TV